Edward Coppinger

Copyright © Edward Coppinger with Katie Coppinger, 2012.
All rights reserved.
The moral right of the author has been asserted.

Published by Edward and Katie Coppinger - July 2013

No part of this book may be reproduced or transmitted in any form or by any other means without permission in writing from the author, except by a reviewer who wishes to quote brief passages in connection with a review written for insertion to a magazine, newspaper or broadcast.

The Poacher's Son

Memories of Ireland and Other Poems

Contents

The River Search	1
The Man from Cluainboo	3
Memories of Our Village Lane	5
The Drovers	8
Lost Love	10
The Poacher's Son	14
Spalpeens	17
The Ploughboys Lament	19
Paddy Baccach	22
Death of a Liner	24
Letterfrack	26
Lackagh Lisheen	27
Ballina (The Clock Maker)	29
River Clare	31
Burial at Sea	34
Cruel Coppinger	37
Jumping the Budget	40
The Hangar Dance	43
Lackagh Castle	45
The Hurricane	47
Teac Mor and Knockdoe Hill	49
The Battle of Knockdoe	51
Wild Geese	54
The Banshee of Cahereenlea	55
The Connaught Rangers	57
A Soldiers Mass	59
Arctic Patrol	63

The QE2 Sailing to the Falklands	67
In Memoriam	69
London Underground Police	72
The Grave of Percy French	75
The Polish Migrant in Ireland	77
The Old Mower	79
The Burieal Barna	81
The Hunt	83
The Dead of Knockmoy Abbey	86
The Ghost of Bodmin Moor	88
Brother Basil	90
My Cottage Ruin	91
The Leprechaun of Puttachaun	94
The Coiste Bower	98
Craogh Patrick	100
The Wind from Glennascaul	103
The Python has it's Day	105
Flanders Trains	107
The Somme Widow	109
Sounds of Youth	111
St Bernards Well of Knockroe of Old	113
Lackagh of My Youth	115
Food for Thought	118

The Poacher's Son is a collection of poems by Edward Coppinger. Born in Galway, Ireland, some of his work reflects his memories of the villages and people he left behind. Other poems are inspired from his service years in the Army, Navy and in the British Transport Police. He lives in Hampshire, England.

The River Search

It was the sky made our river grow,
Faster and faster became its flow,
From the teeming heavens came
A deluge of torrential rain.

Higher and higher rose a flood
Of water that brought no good,
As high as no one could compare
A demon became the river Clare.

Its powerful force was hell bent
In menacing malevolent evil intent –
With angry foaming churning water,
Took the life of John James's daughter.

Older men would often relate
About a curse in that rivers spate,
And of misfortune bringing tears –
Taking life every seven years.

On the banks wet and wild
Vigil was kept for the missing child,
A search machine placed on the deep –
Was a blessed candle on a sheaf!

Prayers and Blessing said and done
The ancient ritual then begun,
And from the safety of the side
The sheaf was launched on the tide.

Floating fast then slowing down,
Beyond Lackagh bridge to Salmontown,
And in the current rapids change,
Quickly passed the bridge of Grange.

Drifting beneath Cregmore bridge,
Strange and surreal its pilgrimage,
At a slow meandering pace
To find grim Clare's hiding place.

Then thrice the sheaf spun round and round
Over deep and dark pol domain –
That God's hand did guide and steer,
Her young body was found here.

In a graveyard below the hill
By the ruins of Columcille,
Once stood a lonely wooden cross
Telling the story of her loss.

Our old men are no longer there,
They sleep now by the Clare,
Who knew well our rivers tears,
That took life every seven years!

The Man from Cluainboo

Sir William Blake was a horseman of fame
All County Galway knew him by name,
He hunted the fox the deer and the hare
Over his lands on the Barony of Clare.

A formidable rider and Master of Hound,
Rode his grey charger to Turlough fairground,
Stating "I challenge anyone to a race fair and square,
May the best man win at Turloughmore Fair".

Daring that wager which no one could take
Too famous the skill of Sir William Blake,
Many would like to, but no one dare do,
Then a voice in the crowd – a Fahy from Cluainboo.

Said Fahy "I have a mare fast and fleet,
And she'll race your stallion right off his feet".
Blake took the challenge saying "Starter, your flag,
I'll soon put a Stop to that little black nag"!

Twice around the Green that was the bet
Through parts which were flooded and soaking wet,
Great cheering and shouting then split the air,
"They're off" was the cry at Turloughmore Fair.

The horses had style the riders had brawn
As they wheeled to the right near Puttachaun,
But slowly ahead Sir William drew
Leaving behind, the man from Cluainboo.

The crowds fell silent not a peep from the sheep,
Just drumming hooves of fast horses feet,
The drink tents were empty there was no ballyhoo,
All eyes were fixed on the man from Cluainboo!

Then Fahy let her go and started to gain
And then went ahead by Cullinanes demesne;
Again level pegging neck and neck once more,
It was one hell of a race at Turloughmore!

At last Blake was beaten a fact he well knew
By a man from the bogs down near Cluainboo,
For the poor horses great was the strain,
Tough was the going on fairground terrain.

But that gallant horse would never run again,
She fell on her knees and died there and then,
And Fahy her owner wept bitter tears,
As quiet with sorrow watched the sightseers.

Then up strode Sir William a man good and true,
Who picked up the hand of the man from Chuainboo,
Saying "good and bad luck you've had today,
Here are the reins, you take my grey"!

There maybe an element of fact in this Ballad.

Memories of Our Village Lane

I remember well our village lane,
Where we walked in youthful years,
And also to the joy and pain,
Of times that were Austere.

Between cold grey stone walls,
Went people of olden ways,
Some still wore Western shawls,
And spoke a Tongue of other days,

Where our forefathers feet once trod,
With the skill they had known
Tilled and worked their fertile sod –
Our fields with crops were sown.

When from high storms lashed,
Inside barns safe from rain
Corn with flails was thrashed
And saved the golden grain.

On the road with cattle and sheep,
To the fair as dawn was nigh,
While the world was fast asleep,
We walked to Athenry.

Oh, that acrid smell of smoke
Where the blacksmiths anvil rung
Into the heart of burning coke –
He thrust his metal tongs.

I remember mornings fresh and sharp,
Stones ringing to hobnailed boots,
Again was playing that Immigrants harp –
"Adieu the nations golden youth".

Where now the Boys we hurled
Against – in our field playing spots
Are they buried around the world,
Are the fields just building plots?

Behind the hearse that took our dead
We followed; words of grief unspoken,
By mourners – with lowered heads –
All knowing their hearts were broken.

Cows looked on at our corteges
With a sad and mournful eye
And we then of tender ages,
Believed they also said Goodbye.

For the dead we'd never see again,
Though maybe young in years,
Knew well our village older men
Too, were holding back the tears.

The Drovers

A herd of cattle from Galway fair
Driven through Oranmore,
Off to the plains of Meath and Kildare,
By legendry Drovers of yore.

These droving kind were hardy and bold
And of God or man unafraid,
Their home was the road in hot or cold,
The warriors of the droving brigade.

Tough robust men with red rosy cheeks,
All things took in their stride,
With no thought of blankets and sheets –
Their bed was the dusty roadside.

Porter they drank by gallon or quart
Without inhibition worry or care,
Fighting regarded as good sport,
Yet looked after their charges Welfare.

Sometimes locked up for the night
Following a fistfight or brawl,
Given bed in a place without light,
That Galwaymen called a Blackhole!

These green Samurai from under the sky,
Of no one were they afraid,
Famous stockmen from days gone by,
And were the talk of Western fairs.

Oh those drovers were real Irish Rovers,
And cattlemen beyond compare,
Their lifestyle long since over –
Our men from the plains of Kildare.

Lost Love

Often I helped her milk the cow
At evening time of day,
Ashamed that I didn't know how,
At her farm near Monivea.

Rooks overhead in listless flight
Homeward on their weary way,
To sleeping nests for the night
In the trees of Monivea.

Around us swallows flying low
As I watched her from nearby,
Signs of rain, she told me so,
And to the cow sang a lullaby.

The cow's side she used to emboss
From a bucket high with foam,
With milky fingers make a cross,
Thence over the Stiles to home.

Young and innocent we were then,
In a Garden of Eden some used to say,
And we too committed that sin –
The snake was also in Monivea!

In our youth such love was shame,
People whispered, "in the family way",
Disgracing her name I was held to blame
For leading a young girl astray.

Not once did our love falter,
In the Scandal that became our lot,
But when denounced from the Altar,
Knew someone had lost the plot.

I heard the sound of a distant drum
With the bugle's call as well,
And a soldier lad did become
Bidding Galway a sad farewell.

I fought in jungle and desert sand
And many a warring foray,
Yet part of my soul that was Ireland –
Kept calling me back to Monivea.

Bitter the wind from Knockbrack,
Colder still the driven rain,
That blew along the Graveyard track,
And through my Zimmer frame.

I knelt beside the cold damp earth
Where she and my son lay,
Her life ending at his Stillbirth,
When I was far from Monivea.

I wish I had seen our child of sin
Who didn't know the day,
And will never walk in sweet Tiaquin,
Or the lovely bogs of Monivea.

I bought a Ring in a distant land
Her name on it was engraved,
In sixty years knew not a hand –
And placed it on her grave.

I exorcised my sorrow and pain,
And swear to God on high,
Clear and plain, the voice the same –
Once more heard that Lullaby.

The Poacher's Son

On Clare's banks at evening time
When the toil of day is done,
And gone are men of rod and line,
Come I the poachers son.

I know so well that rivers mood
Where I 'fished' in sun and rain,
Salmon and trout are food
For me in the poaching game.

I see in water fast and deep
With pools dark as night,
Where wary salmon sleep
And trouts that rise to bite.

I know the moon at harvest-tide
That migrating eels knew as well,
When heavens light was their guide
About which no man could tell.

We stalked our river far and wide
And he taught me the poachers skill,
As I bore that spear by his side
And drunk the poaching thrill.

In old age as death was near
And life's course almost run,
Gave me his precious spear –
To me that poachers son.

I will keep my father's spear
That salmon spear is mine,
And I will give to my son dear,
When ends my earthly time.

For they who made that deadly prong
And anvil that gave it shape,
In the fight for Irelands wrong
Made pikes in Ninety-eight.

Now at night is that river quiet,
Are salmon there still leaping?
Anymore eelers bobbin lights,
Do I hear old poachers weeping?

Spalpeens

Patiently they stood by that Church gate
Groups of Spalpeens for hire await,
Hiring Sunday will start today
For Connemara men in homespun grey.

From bogland and lake of the twelve bens
From rocks and heather in misty glens,
From Carna, Letterfrack and Carraroe
Arrive to harvest the great potato.

Their tongue was Irish no other they knew
Sons of the Gaelthact honest and true,
In homespun clothing called braideen
Badge and hallmark of Galway Spalpeens.

When mass is ended bargaining commence
They're offered pounds shillings and pence,
Hard were the deals not a soft touch
Just fair wages, they never got much.

When all is settled there may be drinks
Tomorrow they'll work amongst Kerr Pinks.
Well did they labour in rocky terrain
In gale force winds, hailstone and rain.

From Connemara they walked all the way
On high roads and bye roads of Galway,
Western bog roads were stony and hard
Through dreary Moycullen and Oughterard.

No fuss was made where they laid their heads
In barns, lofts and at times cowsheds.
At other places too at the end of day
They just curled up in cocks of hay.

At mention of Spalpeens people show unease
That ancestors once worked on their knees.
The opposite is true, it should be said aloud,
" I come from Spalpeens of that I'm proud".

Stories to us they sometimes told
Of magic and battles in days of old,
In the language and tongue of ancient Gaels
Were told and retold these golden tales.

Connemara men were tough as they were kind
Were the real Irish from the 'side behind'.
We won't see them again or their braideen
Forever they're gone our Galway Spalpeens.

Note: Spalpeens: Seasonal workers mostly potato harvesters from Connemara
Kerr Pinks: Late potatoes
Side Behind: Connemara side of Galway city
Church gates: here hiring often took place
Gaelthact: Irish speaking

The Ploughboys Lament

My old plough lies rusting
Beneath a hawthorn tree,
That once I used trusting,
The horses – plough – and me.

Coulter and sock like silver shone
And mouldboard too did sheen,
These parts long since gone,
It's skeleton now obscene.

No more music from my plough
Tilling the green leyland,
No one's able to use it now
No more a human hand.

The joy of that first furrow,
With garters tight below the knee,
'Twas straighter than an arrow
When I ploughed in Gleann Bhui.

I remember the cold bitter wind
Of bracing 'old cows days',
Hardy seagulls dancing behind
A flurry of cabaret displays.

I also thought of Ned and Ted
Who pulled the plough for me,
Measured was their even tread,
When ploughing in Gleann Bhui.

Loyal and true were the two –
Irish draughts was their race,
Well they knew what to do
When straining at the trace.

To them I often used to talk,
And not ashamed to say so now,
Sometimes it was a lonely walk
Behind the moving plough.

On the day they went away,
To Ned and Ted a sad "Goodbye",
I choked on words to say
At the horse-fair in Athenry.

That day too my time came,
For adieu to my native land,
And at the Station got a train –
No plough to feel my hand.

It hid tears and pain that steam train
And loud, loud, the Porters cry,
"For Cork and Limerick junction – change –
Change here at Athenry".

I shut the gate to memories mind,
And quietly tip toe from Gleann Bhui,
The rusting past in fields behind,
Of horses – plough – and me.

Paddy Bacach

I was born on the roadside
At a place called Coilte Macracad,
The whole of Connaught knew me
As poor old Paddy Bacach.

I served my time in the Tinsmiths trade
Mending pots and pans,
Which I can't do anymore –
It's the Arthritis in my hands.

I'm old and feeble now
And lonely on my own,
My family are all in England,
And have a settled home.

They'll never know the freedom
Of an Irish country road,
Or live as their forefathers did,
Who had no fixed abode.

Today we'll go to Lackagh
And camp near Knockdoe,
Tomorrow it could be Athenry,
Coshla, or Knockroe.

At Abbeyknockmoy we'll stay
For a week to kill,
Then go on to Turloughmore,
Going over Annagh Hill.

Oh fond memories I have
Of Ballinasloe Fair days,
Then the travelling life was good,
On them old byways.

I lost my dear wife Alice,
Long long before her time,
And we buried her poor body,
In the graveyard at Ballindine.

Never again on cold roadsides,
Will sound my tinsmiths last,
While stood my faithful donkey
Chomping on the grass.

Soon we'll be united again
In that graveyard in Mayo,
No more in my donkey and cart –
No more fairs in Ballinasloe.

Death of a Liner

Where meets the waters of Itchen and Test
Waits a great Liner for final rest,
Sad and neglected in her last sleep
Finished with sailing, home from the deep.

Destined for death by Shipbreakers hammer,
No more cruises, voyages or passenger glamour;
As she was born so now she must die,
Out in the East under an alien sky.

At her launching how they shouted and cried,
As she slid down the blocks on Lagan side;
High on the halyard with ensign aquiver
So handsome she looked sailing downriver.

Passengers long gone her crew paid off,
She's forlorn and silent on a dark wharf,
All over her deck and rusting hull
Lie white droppings of the predatory gull.

Her hearses have arrived she'll go dignified,
These Tugs will tow her on the noontide.
Gone the hoarse siren that once wakened night
Around Southampton water and Isle of Wight.

She knew the roaring forties and horse latitudes
The Kiel canal, Panama and Suez.
Her joy was sailing to foreign lands,
Soon she will die on Karachi sands.

Oh for the beauty that once she had been
　　　Yet in old age still looks a queen,
And they who welcomed her often before,
Now wave her goodbye from Netley shore.

Letterfrack

In Letterfrack are lonely graves,
All around the wind is sighing
And no one kneels and prays,
For the dead no one is crying.

Fall down gentle Irish rain
From the Bens high above,
Wash away the shame and pain,
Of them who knew no love.

Where there is no cross or plaque,
Nor stone that bears a name,
The place that was our *Gulag*,
Oh great our Nations shame.

Pray for them without a stone
Or without a marble plaque,
Remember, remember, by word alone –
A word called Letterfrack.

Iar Connacht hills keep vigil
On them until Judgement day.
Where the Innocent lie in sleep,
And no one kneels to pray.

They who did good and bad
And both in God's name,
In holy cloth were clad –
Not holy, not holy – but Profane.

Lackagh Lisheen

Quietly we were buried in the middle of night,
With unopened eyes that never saw light
Wrapped in a blanket, sack or praisceen,
They buried our bodies in Lackagh Lisheen.

How strange the plight of us born dead
No Christian service no rosary said,
How lonely and sad can nobody tell
We don't go to heaven, don't go to hell.

No headstone or cross tells of our fate,
No place of death, no name or date,
This is our Limbo that place in between,
Forever we'll lie in this Lackagh Lisheen.

Unbaptized unblessed in the folds of the earth,
In the arms of death at our time of birth,
No separate life did we ever know
Only this cold field here in Knockdoe.

Flowers were not put on our little graves
Just cattle and sheep about us graze,
We cannot have known what's wrong or right
We the dead born who never saw light.

Please let us stay on in eternal sleep
Amongst all those cattle, amongst all the sheep.
Remember that stable of long, long ago
We too are being watched here in Knockdoe.

For all eternity with blue babies as well
We'll never know heaven, we'll never know hell;
This is our Limbo the place in between,
We dead babies in Lackagh Lisheen.

Lisheens: Where stillborn and unbaptised babies were buried, often at night.
There were several Lisheens in Lackagh parish.
There were no Church or religious services.
A Praisceen is an apron made of sacking.

Ballina (The Clockmaker)

It was County Mayo I was born in,
Under the sign of a Horologist star,
At dawn on a cold frosty morning
Near to a town called Ballina.

I roamed the byways of Connaught
Practising my clockmakers art,
The skill of my hands all sought –
They knew I was good at my craft.

Odd kinds I stripped to pieces
Their repairs I took in my stride,
And still on some Mantelpieces,
My work is regarded with pride.

Clocks that never had a name,
While others made Cuckoo calls –
Some keeping time by pulling a chain
And known as Wag 'o' the Walls.

Oh I got them to sing – just a new spring,
And some only given a shake,
The joy when again they'd ring –
Not once did I make a mistake!

Very often in lonely old farms
I've seen watches of solid gold,
With pieces that no longer alarmed,
And often encrusted in mould!

I've worked on clocks sad and forlorn
Their insides long in decay,
Made years before I was born,
When I left – were ticking away!

Timepieces stopped for bereavements –
It's said some never worked again,
That to me of experience
Was something I couldn't explain.

No longer are Journeymen clockmen,
On roads of the kingdom of Conn,
In their fond memory whisper Amen,
Their times in Ireland – long gone.

Peter Cawley, known as Ballina, was a travelling or Journeyman Clockmaker who came from that town and well known in Co. Galway

River Clare – The River of My Youth

Where falls the Irish rain and the west winds blow,
that's where I was born in the county of Mayo.
Among the rocks and heather I rise clean and pure,
in the sky the curlews cry above that purple moor.
I flow along getting strong turning here and there,
still a little stream, but soon the river Clare.

Trout and eel I start to feel my water they explore
as I quicken the pace and forward race heading for Dunmore.
Near the coots nest and mallards rest is where I meander,
with now and then a water hen or wild goose and gander.
That mill wheel I once did feel turned by my power,
farmer's brought their corn and I ground it into flour.

By my banks ancient Irish toiled their lives away,
and ruined castles say to me "we also had our day".
Many are my secrets since life itself began,
plunder war and murder, and many a drowned man.
I had my moments too of trouble strife and hassle,
Cromwell's men washed in me at Claregalway castle!

The town of Tuam fills me with gloom so I move and sally
with waters fast and deep next will be Corbally.
The huntsman's hounds here abound I can hear them still
and the vixen who drank my waters she became their kill.
In olden days this was bog with turloughs all around
where native celts chased the elk with that great wolfhound.

Between Cahernahoon and that famous Lackagh tip head,
The starving hands that cut through rock became the famine dead.
At that time of infamy and days that were so cruel
low was the pay at sixpence a day and a bowl of gruel.
My speed at Lackaghbeg is the fastest I can attain
and near that Grange footbridge, lurks the fishing crane.

Old and lovely is Cregmore bridge with its arches eight,
I love to dash under them when flooding in full spate.
Around the Kiltrogue Lisheen I think of all within,
and sofly cry flowing by for they that knew no sin.
After that bloody fight on the hillside of Knockdoe,
wounded men waded in and cleaned in my flow.

At ruined Claregalway Abbey I heard the monks at prayer
sounding over my waters in the frosty morning air.
Well I knew that holy place when the world was young,
Oh how clear and beautiful were the Te Deums that they sung.
Through gaping windows without their leaded panes
dives the hunting swallow out to pouring rains.

The gobain saors trademark, the famous two tailed cat
now is the living place of the twisting turning bat.
Through the broken doorways where people flocked to mass
are now unkempt graves and wild untended grass.
Oh what things I have seen since time itself began,
plunder, war and murder and many a drowned man.

Humans will never know my secrets, that I truly swear,
I will still be flowing on when they are no longer there.
Flow on and on river Clare you really were our Nile,
great was your bounty to us – to us who only stayed awhile.
Fond memories we have of happy days back then,
fond memories of lost youth, the memories of old men.

Burial at Sea

Roused before dawn with few words said,
Soon we learned it was a service for Dead,
Astern was Africa her coast now a speck
As the funeral party assembled on deck.

Night not yet gone but a new day is nigh,
A time to be born and a time to die,
Over a Stretcher the ensign is draped
With the outline, of a bodily Shape.

Engines are silent the ship has no motion,
Just lapping waves of this wide Ocean,
Each mans thought as he stared at the sea –
Each one thinking, "it could have been me".

A few short prayers the Padre read,
"One day the sea will give up its dead";
The firing party's volley in unison crash,
Some said that was to silence the Splash!

Subdued the Last Post echoed over the foam
The last Goodbye to one we had known,
All of us who had looked death in the eye,
Just stared ahead – Soldiers don't cry.

The propellers re-throb, once more underway,
Death on a 'Trooper' won't cause delay,
Long did we look at our track and Wake
As the Eastern sky lit the daybreak.

Quiet and subdued we to return to sleep,
The Padres words repeating "confined to the Deep",
He said also the dead would again rise,
But nobody believed it, you could see in their eyes.

Plain was the Service over watery graves,
No flowers or wreaths were thrown on the waves.
Oh how we longed for our distant home shore,
For a young soldier, that would be – never more.

Note: It was the custom on Troopships to hold burials at sea more or less in the middled of the night so as not to upset other passengers.
There was a minimum service. This event was in the mid 1950's.

Cruel Coppinger

Loud the gale which has been blowing all night,
The moon and stars in the heavens are bright,
Now is the time when smuggling takes place
There's a contraband ship off Harty Race.

Men and packhorses are at Steeple Brink
Where hardy smugglers are landing the drink;
No Excise or Gaugers are out on the wave
They'll hide and stow it in Coppingers cave.

Around this headland where westerlies roar
No honest Cornishman dare open his door;
They fear Cruel Coppinger that nasty Brigand,
The terror of the sea, the curse of the land;
He had a fast schooner Black Prince by name,
The greatest freebooter of this westerly main.

Dread of this pirate filled people with gloom
The scourge of Hartland he lived at Welcombe;
An Irish villian in these parts held sway,
From where the Tamar is born to Hartland bay.
For Coppinger was cruel, as cruel as could be,
The curse of the land the curse of the sea.

Tonight is the night smugglers have fun
With barrels of Brandy, Gin and red Rum.
Silent they move with casks on their backs
Through fields and dales on Coppingers tracks.

The booze will be stashed in that craggy enclave
Known to Cornish as Coppingers cave,
A hole in the cliff one hundred feet down
Unseen and unnoticed by men of the Crown;
For government agents in cliff tops hide
Awaiting harvest on the incoming tide.

It was Coppingers law west of the Tamar,
In this wild land unknown to the stranger:
Here was a coast where wrecks were fair game
And throats cut in many a lane;
Excise and Gaugers worked at great risk
For smugglers justice was silent and brisk!

This buccaneer who brought suffering and pain
Was called in Cornwall, Coppinger the Dane;
He came by water from lands far away
And left in the same manner near Hartland Bay;
His descendents still live in the town of Roscoff
Where passengers from England roll on and off! *

In Hartland now there are no smugglers or wreckers
Just jogging Germans and young pony trekkers.
On nights when storms lash Gull Rock
People hear sounds of bottles and crock,
These ghostly smugglers, Cruel Coppinger as well
Are emptying their barrels in some boozy hell.
For Coppinger was cruel, as cruel as could be
The curse of the land the curse of the sea.

*John Coppinger left Cork about 1760 and lived in Roscoff returning there after Cornwall. His name is Danish. The Coppingers came to Ireland as Vikings. The paths used by his smugglers were known as Coppinger tracks. The Cave is still there. The family traded between Cork and Roscoff His family history is well documented. He probably stayed away from France during the Revolution. The family had business or estates there, and returning when it was safe. *Day trippers, Booze Cruises!*

Jumping the Budget

Near the town of Gort I was born,
At a place called Killgannion,
Where I fell in love with a travelling girl,
Known as Crissie Bannion.

Her father was a cruel man,
He was cruel to me,
Cruel to his faithful wife
And also poor Crissie.

When I asked him for her hand
To be my life's companion,
He said "Young man you'll never wed,
Or take to bed –
My daughter Crissie Bannion".

Said Crissie "let's run away
For to elope and marry,
We'll meet tonight in bright moonlight
By my camp in Ballinderry.

I must have a wedding white
With all the festive trimming",
Until I told her we were very poor
And didn't have a penny.

To Mayo she said we should go
And on foot trudge it,
Like travellers of long ago
There 'jump the budget'.

Happily we walked the roads
In warm Spring sunshine,
Light was our budget loads,
As we skipped through Ballindine.

Where the fairies danced at night
Beneath a blackthorn tree,
In the early morning light
I married dear Crissie.

It was in a sacred place
Once a fairy ring,
To the music of the blackbird
And beautiful did he sing.

No people in good suits
Or clergy in vestments white,
When we 'jumped the budget'
In that secret travellers rite.

How we leaped and laughed
As over the packs we flew,
Repeating words and signs
That only travellers knew.

Oh, the magic of that morning
Nobody there to stare,
Just the singing blackbirds
And a curious mountain hare.

I went back once more
When she passed away,
To put flowers on the spot
Where was our wedding day.

When suddenly there was music
That filled the fairy ring,
Once more it was a blackbird
And for me, She began to sing.

Jumping the Budget was a form of marriage used by travellers throughout the British Isles. Recently at Glastonbury in Somerset there has been an upsurge.

The Hangar Dance

Let me stand again on Galway's strand,
Listenening to music of a Ceilidh band,
Borne on breezes across Salthill
That poignant sound of Ballinakill.

Once more I'll dance the Siege of Ennis,
Abhorring the smell of pungent Guinness,
It's my last time Hangar, please let me in,
To remember the lad I was back then.

There will be girls I took on the floor,
Geraldine and Catherine from Oranmore,
And lovely redhead Peggy O'Malley,
Who was from Cortoon or maybe Lavally.

Eileen I'll meet on the Promenade walk,
In the Connemara tongue she used to talk,
Our language was laughter and good enough,
Under the stars and sound of surf.

An all night Ceilidh always good fun
From late Sunday evening to rising sun,
Youth at the dance came from all over,
Menlo, Moylough to beyond Cloughanover.

How we ducked, turned, stomping and wheeling,
Until as was said – our heads were Reeling!
Sometimes as if to liven up the night
Pushing shoving and maybe a fight.

An army of cyclist's going home without lights,
Through the city of Tribes at end of night,
Raucous and loud, a ragged cavalcade,
To Gardai – 'The charge of the no light Brigade'!

Other nights too, that were dark as pitch,
We'd waken the dead of Two Mile Ditch!
Castlegar dogs were mean nasty packs,
Their watchkeeping done from under the stacks.

They knew well about Haggard romance
And what we'd get up to – given the chance.
Like missiles streaked down Holmes's hill,
Ahead lay Claregalway slumbering still.

In fields and meadows sung the Corncrake,
Telling the world of coming daybreak.
With night almost gone homeward we jog –
In a couple of hours it's off to the bog.

That Irish music is with me still
I will never forget you Ballinakill.
No more green Hangar by Salthills seas,
Thank you old dance hall – for the Memories.

Lackagh Castle

Bruised and battered this fort of stone
Proud undefeated, survives alone,
Solid as rock on which it stands,
At birth shaped by a Masters hand.

That Masons skill and craft so fine,
Between the stones hardly a join,
His handsome art and strength of will
On ancient walls we see still.

A beacon of days long passed away
Elevated and haughty in decay,
Witness to mankind's hopes and fears
His folly, laughter, toil and tears.

The place sentries did vigil keep
In and out starlings sweep,
From their nests perched on high,
The sinister mocking jackdaws cry.

No longer heard on echoing walls
The martial blast of bugle calls;
Or at end of day in evenings still,
The tolling Angelus from St. Columcille.

Where a Ceolain played his harp
All now empty, silent – stark.
The Pipers lament sad and shrill,
Sounds no more up Lackagh Hill.

Stories as well never to be told,
Of fights and strife in times of old,
This limestone bastion battle withstood,
Where Irish and stranger shed their blood.

Castle people then did command
Unbeaten people in a beaten land,
In bog, wood, or moorland track,
The proud invader had to watch his back.

Dangerous it was in boreens green,
Where lurked assassins unknown unseen,
From that grey tower in the sky
A watch was kept on passers-by.

On men and beasts with their daily load
On a track that was Lackagh road,
And Monks also passed this way
Between Abbeyknockmoy and Claregalway.

Stranger too when you pass this way,
Think of Irish people from another day,
All long gone, most unknown,
Our nation's history – is that stone.

The Hurricane

Mighty the force of that lashing sea,
The rigging trembled and moaned,
In mountainous waves as none did see,
On an ocean that boiled and foamed.

That hurricane's blast shook the mast,
The decks were out of bounds,
And men thought of sins long past –
In the 'eye' of the storms sound.

We pitched, rolled twisted and tossed,
Like a cork on maddened seas,
Some said "we're as good as lost",
And spoke to God on knees.

Crockery stashed broke loose and smashed,
All hell was unleashed below,
As downward waves onboard crashed –
Each threatened a mortal blow.

All our thoughts were in unison
At each dangerous breaking wave,
And spoke for all the Bosun,
Saying "for us it's a watery grave".

The Angel of death was about that night,
We felt his beating wings,
And waited white, numb with fright,
In dread of his deadly sting.

When that awful wind was done,
And slow came the dawning day,
Some also looked at the rising sun,
And to that God too did pray.

Grateful now to have won the fight,
And our ship still making way,
Damaged she was, yet watertight –
All thoughts of God – we stowed away.

Teac Mor and Knockdoe Hill

Is Teac Mor there anymore,
In my mind I see it still,
Where in youth we did explore,
On top of Knockdoe hill?

When as boys we chased the hare
To the place where no birds sung,
Into that lonely pile did dare
In days when we were young.

Where the Banshee's cry was heard
And brave men paled in fright,
And braver too were perturbed
By that demon of the night.

Are there yet piles of stones
Where under rests the slain,
Now old green decayed bones
For long in Death's domain?

From that house sad and grey
Was Lough Corrib seen so clear,
On a fine day too Galway Bay,
With Connemara looking near.

Is there still a secret hollow
Where Penal Masses were said,
Did the faithful pray and follow
To the altar on a primrose bed?

That old hill is calling me
Oh I hear it soft and low,
"Come back once more and see
Me – once more before you go".

"I cannot go now Knockdoe
I am old weary and ill,
Not like I used to long ago;
But I promise – my Ashes will".

The Battle of Knockdoe
19th August 1504

Oh mother dear soon you'll hear, on this earth I am no more,
In the ranks of death I will be, in a grave near Turloughmore;
This earth I share with others, lads hardly grown,
Forever we'll lie beneath the sky at a place called Ballyabrone.

Curse the day they passed this way and urged us all to go,
To join a fight that was not our right, on a hill called Knockdoe;
Proudly marched these armed men, as rank and rank passed by
I followed horse and gallowglass and joined up in Athenry.

Brightly shone the autumn sun, 'twas a beautiful morn,
Cheerfully did harvesters wave from their fields of corn.
There were men from Mayo, and many more from Clare,
Some just had knives and sticks and lots of feet were bare.

Arrayed in lines for battle on that slope towards south east
Our battle cry rent the sky that would frighten man and beast;
Ready was the enemy with battleaxe bow and spear
As slowly and inexorably our fighting lines drew near.

Loudly clashed steel on steel, and bowmen let the arrows fly,
So many were released they darkened out the sky,
We rushed charged pushed and cut, and battled to and fro
Red became that emerald field at the battle of Knockdoe.

Arrows caused the greatest loss to infantry and pikemen
Thus we lost the heart, lost the fight, and the will to win;
The foe fought us well, their courage carried them the day,
And we beaten Connaught men fled in disarray.

Numerous were the fallen who lay in awful gore,
Many wounded died at Laughtgeorge and Turloughmore,
At Ballyabrone and Kiltrogue were buried in graves amass
Friend and foe rich and poor under Irish grass!

Much is said of the glory of Clanricardes name
But we the slain and fallen do not to that acclaim.
There will come a time when wars and battles cease
And Ireland will at long long last gain rightful peace.

So mother dear, when the news you hear, don't shed tears or cry,
Just leave me here in Ballyabrone, far from Athenry;
Come other times, come other days of us no one will know,
Future men will not speak again; of the Battle of Knockdoe.

There is not any historical evidence that gunpowder was used in any significant amount at Knockdoe; the main reason for the high casualties may have been the longbow. Following the battle, the hands of dead pikemen, were found to be pinned to pike handles by the downward plunge of arrows. Longbow arrows were as big as broom handles with nasty metal attachments. It was common to have three in the air at different heights so all landed together, and at the same time. For unprotected, untrained Irishmen they were lethal.

Wild Geese

Cold's the wind of the frozen north
Where the sun has slipped away,
Time for geese to sally forth
And seek the longer day.

On following winds southward wing,
It's a race that must be run,
Tunes of north on wings they sing,
From lands that have no sun.

Now far behind the Arctic lands,
Through clouds that hide the sky,
Obeying the ganders flight commands
To the warmer south they fly.

Above field and lake they navigate,
Over mist and fogs snow white,
By land and sea orientate –
And by stars that shine at night.

Countless miles of gruelling flight,
Until their wearying trek is done,
Seeking the place of more daylight
From lands that have no sun.

The Banshee of Cahereenlea

Hard was the frost with a cold winds bite
Cycling to Turloughmore on a dark winters night,
Homing from a dance at the town of Monivea,
With a song in my heart down Cartymore way.

By the wild waters of Turlough Ban sea,
With billowing waves that rolled towards Rathfee!
What I heard first I can never explain,
A whining sob, or shriek of great pain.

The cold came all over, my hair stood on end,
And I thought it unnatural, cycling the bend,
But knew for sure approaching Cahereenlea,
'Twas the sinister cry of the dreaded Banshee!

A piercing wail and sobbing cauterwaul,
That siren of death from behind a stone wall,
Awful it was full of pathos and sorrow
Freezing my lifeblood, backbone and marrow.

Chilling her lament an eerie cacophony,
Warning of death in Coolarne or Canteeny,
Somewhere nearby a heart would soon break,
By that angel of doom bringing heartache.

She kept pace with me or so I thought,
With this prophet of gloom I had to consort.
I never saw her at all, 'twas just her sad cry,
From front and behind it filled the black sky.

She howled from the sides, and cried from before,
'Til I thought my heart wouldn't take anymore;
With the superstition inbred in my race
I crossed myself thrice, begging Gods grace.

Suddenly there was silence, the strangest hush,
When in front dashed a fox in a desperate rush,
All mangled and broken with a pitiful wail –
The trailing trap told its own gruesome tale.

With the thrill of danger that is surreal,
Oh I wanted my Banshee, I wanted her real,
So my grandchildren could be told on my knee
"I heard her once, I really heard the Banshee"!

Now so long ago it all seems a dream,
That cry of pain and agonizing scream;
It was that poor fox that done it for me,
I no longer believe in the bloody Banshee.

Note: Banshee: Fairy woman who cried warning of death. Never seen, only heard, but not by those who were to die.
Cahereenlea: Had most Banshee activity in Lackagh parish!
Coolarne/Canteeny/Cartymore: Local areas and villages.
Turlough Ban. Flood plain.

The Connaught Rangers – the 88th

Proudly they marched from the Barracks Renmore,
Bound out for service in Bombay or Lahore,.
In front was the band and well did it play
The regimental march, Saint Patrick's Day;
England's greatest regiment, her bravest and best
The great Connaught Rangers, men of the West.

When the troop train from Galway crossed to Athlone
Some sad Rangers had a last look at home;
Well did they know they'd never see more
Their bones would bleach on some foreign shore.
They enlisted in Galway, Mayo and Roscommon
Sligo, Leitrim, and west of the Shannon.

From mountains and lakes and valleys green
They put Gods fear into enemies of the Queen;
'Half of the Road' the regiments motto did say,
For the famous Rangers, ..."get out of the way".
Many had names like Joyce, Burke and O'Connor
Names now found on great Rolls of Honour
Honour cost dear these brave sons of Conn
Their bodies still lie on Marne and Somme.

In battles and wars for hundreds of years,
The Peninsular, India, Transvaal and Armentiers.
Covered in glory and fame so great
Was "Prince Consort Own", the great Eighty Eight.
Boers they fought at Tungelia and Spion Kop
Uphill they charged but few reached the top,
Losses were huge yet they carried the day,
Oh, bitter the tears around Galway Bay.

Indian Sepoys attacked saying "God is great"
And on Ranger steel met a sad fate;
In the Crimea they battled Cossack and cannon
Tough were these soldiers from west of the Shannon.
Gallantry and battle honours too numerous to name
From Sulva in Turkey to Elandsfontein;
Renowned for courage in peril and dangers
When the going was rough, send for the Rangers!

Stood holy Jerusalem with great Rock and Dome,
As holy as the Vatican in the city of Rome,
It's first Christian soldiers for six hundred years,
When the Rangers went in, some shed tears.
They mutineed in India at Jullanders hot sands
Against King and Emperor, against Black and Tans,
Disbanded and scattered the Connaught Rangers no more,
Never again seen around barracks Renmore.

At Windsor Royal Chapel their last Colours rest
And at St Nicholas, Galway, others hang blessed.
'Tis said that some nights on the hill of Carnmore
When winds blow in from Aran and shore,
Ghostly music is heard far out in the Bay,
It's that Regimental March, Saint Patrick's Day.

A Soldiers Mass

Sanctus, Sanctus, the Padre said
And a thousand men bowed the head,
No loud commands or shouted word,
The Mass in latin all understood.

Of different ranks ages and race,
In a land of conflict – a desolate place.
With weapons of war about our feet
The ancient responses did repeat.

Australian men tough and strong
From Wagga Wagga or Dannedong,
Proud Fijians fit and able –
Africans from the Nile's cradle.

Catholics from the Himalayas,
Malaccan Christians of West Malaya,
Irishmen both South and North,
Hardy Scotsmen of Clyde and Forth.

Devout believers from Singapore,
Maori giants of New Zealand's shore.
From his Jeep's altar – a handbell tolled
And the rites of Mass to us he told.

Old veterans of many campaigns
Children once more we became,
Remembering our first Communion day,
Wondering when and where went astray.

Confirmation sacrament all well knew,
Soldiers of Christ – sworn to be true.
Some mindful also of their lapsed souls,
Food for thought when in Foxholes!

When the Lords word to us was read
Was here and there a tear shed,
And thoughts of Masses far away
Where we learned to kneel and pray?

At this solemn rite all were intent,
No blessed candles or incense,
Strange and surreal the atmosphere,
To a man – believed that God was near.

A bond between us soldier men –
The Mass in latin by our Chaplain,
He said, "Ita Missa", in peace go,
At that soldiers Mass of long, long ago.

Arctic Patrol – Royal Navy

Through freezing water amongst the ice floes,
North by north east in storm and snows,
Grey was this arctic so cold and dank,
Tracking submarines out of Murmansk.

Handsome our ship a greyhound of the seas,
Gale force ten she took with great ease,
And packed a hard punch of weaponry might,
In northerly wastes of all day or night.

We young sailors stalwart and bold
Played a great game in a war that was Cold!
Ploughing giant waves foam flecked and green,
With asdics pinging for Soviet submarines.

Around Bear Island and Spitsbergen too,
In this deceptive ocean sometimes peaceful and blue,
Above and below it was a sinister game,
From the Faroes and Iceland, to west of Jan Mayen.

The white-coated boffins who often sailed onboard,
Silent and mysterious, never uttered a Word,
In dark signal cabins eavesdropping the sea,
Ivan to Boris and Yuri, or maybe the KGB!!

This was a place of so called war graves
Unknown uncharted far under the waves,
Where many were sunk in another war,
Does anybody learn from what's gone before?

These war dead vessels now lying on the bottom,
Their convoys and voyages long since forgotten.
To Murmansk in Russia were bound these ships,
What would they now say these long silenced lips?

Surely they'd say their deaths were in vain,
"For you're still playing another war game,
Yesterday our allies, now the enemy-
We don't understand it, us under the Sea".

Strange was this world of all day or all night,
Where lurked the polar bear in his camouflage white.
Practicing manoeuvres with depth charge and mock fights,
Whilst high in the sky flashed the great northern lights.

Where the dreaded U Boat once hunted for prey,
Now flaring oil and gas Rigs light up the way.
No more asdic sounds of grey men of war;
The Cold war is over, Arctic patrols are no more.

Note: *A polar bears normal colour is yellow becoming white in the arctic winter.*
Russians often referred to such activities as 'Games' and were probably right.
War Graves - hundreds of WW2 ships litter the seabed.

The QE2 Sailing to the Falklands From Southampton Docks

They came to the Docks in thousands
By train, by bus or by car
All wanting to view the great QE2
Sail off to the Falklands and war.

Packed was the huge Ocean Terminal
On floors roofs and balconies,
Well did they applaud our young men to war
Going off to fight the 'Argies'.

That fever of war was infectious
Loud did they shout and exhale,
As the mighty ship her moorings did slip
And to the South Atlantic set sail.

How they yelled for Argentine blood;
And for the soldiers who might have to die
Women did a striptease along the quays
That timeworn soldiers goodbye.

If only these docks could speak
All this they had known before,
The flower of our youth cheered by the uncouth
To die on some faraway shore.

Farewell to that great ocean liner
To whom our monarch gave name,
So many were touched by great sadness
Many also felt a great shame.

Strange are our kin in human skin
Some people we don't know at all,
The great hysteria for this Galtieri
As if it all was a game of football.

In that human mass were the top brass
Aloof and upright by the rails,
What with military bands and upraised hands
All that was missing was the Seig Heils!

Lined up on deck were great Regiments
With flags blowing all awry,
Odd it's to say as she sailed away
We didn't know whether to laugh or cry.

Note – Ocean Terminal since demolished,
Galtieri: President of Argentina,
QE2: Commandeered for the Falkland conflict

In Memoriam

Where stormy petrels wing on the tide,
So far away from land alone,
Below this ocean bleak and wide
They lie forgotten unknown.

No passing ship will ensign dip,
Or bugler the Last Post play,
Nor shrill Bosuns pipe of a warship,
Or Padre for their souls pray.

No Celtic cross will tell their loss,
No mother will weep on their graves,
Where great breakers roll and toss;
The Dead – far under the waves.

Over them now let storms rage
In their watery tombs asleep,
Brave brave Mariners of another age,
May they rest forever in peace.

For the Merchant Seamen who lost their lives in the North Atlantic during WWII (including many from the Claddagh, Galway).

London Underground Police

Sometimes at night when I can't sleep
I think I hear trains down in the deep.
I hear muffled whistles with a mournful sound –
And rattling clatter of trains below ground,
Halting at stations, the platform shakes
With that piercing screech of Westinghouse brakes.

We railway cops who worked night and day
Beneath this Metropolis built upon clay,
On Underground stations working beats
Watching commuters flock from the streets,
Thousands and thousands going up and down,
Grim faced lemmings of this London town.

A flotsam and jetsam from the whole human race,
The great family of Adam squeezed into one place,
Of countless faces not one did we know
Like the cold humanity of an indifferent foe;
Amongst teeming peoples and scurrying feet,
In all this city it was the loneliest Beat.

In expressionless faces so much could be read,
Of sorrow and pain, love or just dread;
In and out of trains like a bat out of hell,
Where do they come from or go, could anyone tell?
A heavily covered lady who hailed from Assam,
A camera clicking tourist who came from Japan.

A kilted Scotsman, hungover and cantankerous
We know for sure he got on at St Pancras,
And here is an American from Nebraska State
Who actually said, "aren't English cops great".
We Underground law the Queens peace did keep
In this great artery way down in the deep.

Piccadilly Circus station that name is just right,
The Concourse a ring with a show day and night.
Thronged with sightseers, vagrants and deserters,
Predatory paedophiles and sexual perverters,
Where thieves and pickpockets practice their crafts,
Buskers and hustlers and street walking tarts,
The old the young the wise and silly
Met in this hunting ground here in the 'Dilly'.

The magic of this railway was wonderful to see
Lines under, over, and across the city,
Above and below dear old Father Thames
Where Centurions bathed in Roman times,
Kangaroo valley once called Earls Court
Full with Australians who called everyone 'sport'!
Lonely it was on beats that were grey
Where the sun never shone through the length of the day.

From High Barnet, Morden and Bromley by Bow,
To Watford, Ealing, Wimbledon and Heathrow.
We kept law and order and that royal peace,
We ordinary coppers of the Railway Police,
Hard did we toil by night and by day
Beneath this Metropolis built upon clay.

The worlds' greatest capital with bustle and strife
Underground the system that carries its life.
Fond memories too of days that are done,
Soon time to say, "last train has gone".
How strange it was on beats that were grey
With no sight of the sun through the length of the day,
Oh, that muffled whistle with its mournful sound
And the rattle and clatter of trains under ground.

The Grave of Percy French

In a Formby Churchyard wherein you lie,
Under the grey of a Lancashire sky,
'Tis peaceful and quiet where you abide,
Your last resting place on Merseyside.

Can you still hear the Irish sea surf,
And wish 'twas Roscommon with the smell of turf,
Lying with your kin in their demesnes,
From whence you came, near Elphins plains?

The words on your cross made my heart wrench,
The grave of my idol – poet Percy French.
How I remember that song with love,
'Come back Paddy Reilly to Ballyjamesduff'.

The Band often played 'Phil the Fluters Ball',
Down by Suez and Berlins Wall,
In foreign lands dreary and war torn,
They 'Beat Retreat' to the 'Mountains 'o' Mourne'.

Proudly wearing the Saffron kilt too,
So evocative the pipes of Brian Boru,
And all our hearts burst with pride,
Whether from Shanklin – or the Bogside!

Oh them voices beautiful and clear,
Rendering the air of Abdul Abulbul Amir!
And others too with a Southern brogue,
That moistened our eyes, to Eileen oge!

Where now your family, where now your race,
Are they of great lineage gone without trace,
Who came to our land from the Welsh Marches,
Foremost they were of Strongbows archers.

A lover of Ireland it tells in your Words,
The sadness and poignancy – the funny – the absurd.
"Sleep on Percy by Merseyside's wave –
Where the breath of Ireland blows on your grave".

Brian Boru Pipes – Irish bagpipes

The Polish Migrant in Ireland

They speak to me of sweet Tralee
And lovely lakes of Killarney,
But I know where I'd rather be –
On the slopes of Zakopane.

They tell me too of Galway Bay,
With Irish 'craic' and Blarney,
Whilst I dream of far away,
Of snows on Zakopane.

When I leave grey Athenry
And dear old Ballinasloe,
To home I'll fly where 'tis dry,
And twenty degrees below!

To smell again the Baltic pines
And every day won't be rainy,
Oh, for the cold sun that shines
On the mountains of Zakopane.

Once more to fish under ice
On the mighty frozen Vistula,
For us it will be paradise –
For me and dear Finnula.

A Celtic god told my soul
I heard him say so plainly,
Go home go home, wandering Pole,
Go home to Zakopane!

Goodbye to Irish fields so green
Where winds are wet and stormy,
To home I'll take a nice colleen,
Finnula – to wed in Zakopane.

To see the snow in moonlights glow
With summers dry and balmy,
Where the damp winds do not blow,
On the slopes of Zakopane.

The Old Mower

Once more I'll whet the Blade
And reset the old Scythetree,
Well my father knew that trade,
And taught his skill to me.

When I mow in Gleann Bhui
I'll cut a swathe four feet wide,
As if the scythe were part of me,
Swinging from side to side.

Half a step with a curving sweep,
And the falling corn sings,
The stubble behind one inch deep
By measured skilful swings.

I'll shout to the binding men
If they've stopped to smoke,
And in my father's tongue scold them –
'Twas the Irish then I spoke.

We'll drink the watered oatmeal
To slake the burning thirst
When that blazing heat we feel,
And the sun can do its worst.

The stooks will be in the old way
Just like soldiers in a row,
As was done in my father's day,
When they harvested long ago.

Where stands the lonely Fairy tree
I'll cut carefully by its side
So they don't come to harm me,
When at night they dance and hide.

From olden days that Hawthorn
Has stood midfield on its own,
Since the time of my grandfather –
And will be there when I'm gone.

Oh the swish of mowing steel
Will be music to my ears,
Young and strong again I'll feel
As I was in youthful years.

From my half-door now can see,
Gleann Bhui I mowed in yore,
The legs no longer carry me –
I'll use that Scythe no more.

Scythetree; Poetic name for a scythe especially if the handle was grown to shape in Cregmore coppice wood and the like.

The Burieal Barna

Sometimes from across the waves
Come memories of home once more,
Of my youth and Claddagh days,
By the bay of Galway's shore.

Whence a child and put to sleep,
Dreaming of ships foreign bound,
I heard that foghorns vigil keep,
Through a window came its sound.

At times I wept at its strident bray,
Said mother, "It won't harm yah,
For 'tis a song of Galway Bay,
And called the Burieal Barna".

When mists and fog blocked the sky,
As waves broke on the shore,
I came to love that foghorns cry,
And dreamt of it for evermore.

I answered the call of the sea
As my father had done as well,
And eager for the world to see,
To the Claddagh bid farewell.

Out where great rollers break
The worries of land behind,
My ships track in the wake –
With the smell of saltsea wind.

Around Cape Horn I often sailed
In seas that pitched and tossed,
Where was seen the mighty whale,
And Behind – the Albatross.

I saw the sun rise and set
On the worlds' greatest oceans,
And things too I'll never forget –
In the horror of wars commotions.

Once fogbound at anchor lay,
In the port of Yokohama,
Again I wept for Galway Bay –
'Twas the cry of a Burieal Barna.

Now at night dreams come afar,
So clear they leave no doubt,
Warning soon I must cross the Bar,
That my tide was ebbing out.

No more I'll hear that foghorns tone
Swinging on the tides,
Nor see again my Claddagh home,
Or the City of the Tribes.

And when I sail to seas on high,
To meet my heavenly Karma,
May I hear a last plaintive sigh –
The Song of the Burieal Barna.

Burieal Barna – A local name for a foghorn of Barna, Galway.

The Hunt

Hard rode the Hunt through Cartymore
Baying and howling the hounds went before,
With steam from their breath trailing behind,
As over Knockroe blew an Easterly wind.

Thirsting for blood, the chase and thrill,
Under the Master of Hounds, 'Bold Pickersgill',
A thundering of hooves made the earth shake
By Molly O' Rourke, the Blyths and the Blakes.

Like legendry horses of ancient Greece
They jumped stone walls with wings on their feet,
Great horsemen they were and famous Hellraisers,
The cream of their class – them old Galway Blazers.

Their panting Beagles loudly gave tongue
As from the Huntmaster a "Tally ho" rung;
The pack 'Whipper in' won't let them stray
Seeking the scent around Calereenlea.

They have risen a fox, he's running for life
The villainous creature away in full flight!
Again shrills the horn "Fox in sight"
A chilling sound that filled him with fright.

The great hunting Blazers all wanted him dead,
The denizens of Lackagh had a price on his head,
Galloping full chase – headlong their rush
All wanting his blood, his hide and his brush.

The quarry of the 'meet' was a fox of renown
Oh beautiful he was so handsome and brown,
His eyes were the colour of liquid gold,
He was cunning and clever as he was bold.

He knew every henhouse, pond and hollow
Between Coshla, Grange and Lisheenavalla.
'Twas a glorious sight, a grand Hunting scene,
Towards Coolarne woods all verdant and green.

This Reynard was cute – he had many tricks
And would outsmart they who hunted for kicks;
Smarter than them – smarter by far
Than the likes of Bowes-Daly, or Major Carr.

Crafty he was hiding under a Stack
And when they had passed, fast doubled back,
Twisting and turning through Haggard and garden
Well did he know every inch of Coolarne!

He reached his 'Bolt hole' bizarre and strange
High in the sky at the castle of Grange,
Clawing himself up between ivy and stone,
Through a sanitary shaft that nobody had known.

On top of the greenery thirty feet high
Watched in amusement his tormentors go by,
The Blazers dashed past all still hell bent,
But at Grange Castle at last lost his scent.

Off in the distance near the Clare's flow,
The dispersing call saying 'homeward we go';
Safe and snug it was where the ivy did creep
And Reynard just yawned and went off to sleep!

Some people say when the moon is down low
And cold is the wind from over Knockroe,
Strange hoof-beats are heard across the night sky,
'Tis them old Galway Blazers fox hunting on high!

The Dead of Knockmoy Abbey

Around that ruined house of God
Where the dead are buried deep,
In blessed and sacred sod
Long gone Brothers sleep.

Of them nothing is known
From where or whence they came,
At this great Abbey built of stone –
Men who have no name.

Did they know a woman's love,
Or earthly pleasures enjoy,
Was their reward in heaven above,
The Cistercians of Knockmoy?

They warn us on limestone grey
In words etched with sorrow,
"As we are here today
You will be tomorrow".

They ask prayers for Martin
In Latin or Irish script,
For him long departed
Below his crumbling crypt.

Slumber on royal O'Conor
In your lonely tomb,
For a name of such honour,
Better the ruin and gloom.

You Celtic noble of Red Hand
Your flag now flies high,
A symbol of our divided land,
Ireland – Ireland tell us why?

Bleak and sad in moonlights gleam,
Poignant, under the western sky,
By Abberts gentle flowing stream,
Lie the dead of Abbeyknockmoy.

The Ghost of Bodmin Moor

When day has gone and falls the night,
Over Bodmin Moor the owl's in flight,
Lonely his call that haunting hoot,
As rabbits into their burrows scoot.

While the moon and stars are down
And sleeps the righteous of Bodmin town,
Over this timeless and hallowed land
Stalks the ghost with a Hairy Hand.

Between sunset and break of day,
Around this Moor bleak and grey,
The restless soul of the Hairy Hand –
Comes from a place of lost and damned!

It grabbed the steering wheel of motor cars,
And on motorcycles - 'twas the handlebars;
On lonely tracks where cyclists ride,
At their backsides it sat astride!

Men of Cornwall have courage galore,
Brave they are - but shun the Moor;
And when they've seen it - so they tell,
They cross themselves and run like hell!

Where mighty gales and cold winds howl
The Hairy Hand abroad will prowl,
And Cornish maidens demure and chaste,
Claim they felt its touch about the waist!

Betwixt themselves these maidens say,
"We know what 'twas – "it's one of they".
Mornings light stops ghostly games,
And the Hairy Hand goes back to flames!

Come tourist folk in new track suits
With jolly joggers running Boots,
And when they've seen the hand that's hairy –
Boast they've seen a hairy fairy!

Widely reported in British National newspapers during the autumn of 2008, following many reports of incidents on Bodmin Moor area, Cornwall, concerning a phantom hairy hand.

Brother Basil

Here I lie under an alien sky
Beyond the Irish sea,
Stranger, if you pass by my grave,
Say a prayer for me.

I who served the King and God,
Now in a graveyard facing East,
But, wishing it was another place –
The graveyard at Kilchreest.

You who rest with other Monks
In lines row by row,
What were your thoughts before you left,
Can we the living know?

Did your past flash back before you,
And relive and see it all again,
Was there shame, guilt or fear,
Or some awful hidden pain?

You who ask, will find the answers,
When you are as me,
On earth they cannot be found –
Only here in eternity.

Question not about my fight
Or things I had to do,
The hand of fate is the guiding light,
For me – for them – for you.

Rest in peace Michael, a victim of troubled times in Ireland.

My Cottage Ruin

It's roofless walls bare and sad,
An eyesore some folk say,
The place I was born and bred
And first saw light of day.

Now in briars overgrown,
There's no fireplace anymore,
Long gone the old hearthstone –
The cottage Soul is no more.

Around that hearth men used to say
When storms shook the floor,
And talk as if 'twas yesterday,
Of *Oiche na Gaoithe Moire*.

The wild wind was Gods music then
Playing through poplar trees,
To us in the cosy kitchen
Saying the Rosary on our knees.

At the dying fire we'd stare,
Daydreaming as it was said,
Kneeling against a rickety chair
Or the ancient settlebed.

Into that settle we laid our heads,
Three *Putachs* side by side,
Oh for us 'twas a silky featherbed,
With straw under our backsides!

By the door was a Damascus rose
That never knew a pruners shears,
Beneath our sheepdog used to doze
Whose bark no one did fear.

The peaceful scenes from that door
Was our Galway long ago –
Coolarne, Grange and Cregmore,
And the heather of Knockroe.

Is my memory tricking me,
Surely I can't hear still
A stuck pigs squeal in Cantoney –
Can be heard on Lackagh hill?

The wild ducks calling out on high
Seeking floodwater of the Clare,
Their drake leading from the sky
His call also saying – "Beware".

That cottage rang with laughter,
And was no stranger to the tears,
We never thought of the hereafter,
In our happy childhood years.

The Leprechaun of Puttachaun (*A Monologue*)

When I left that Turloughmore pub
'Twas a clear and starry night,
I wasn't what you'd call plastered
More what you say a 'bit tight'!

I went on the road towards Coolarne
The one that goes to Athenry,
With a camog under my arm
And a stagger or two won't deny!

And there on the roadside at Puttachaun
Calmly sitting on the grass,
Was the tiniest sweetest leprechaun
With a face as bold as brass!

He was working away on a shoe
'Half soles' I'd say he was stitching,
He was good I'll give him his due
For me it was kind of bewitching!

Says I to him "God Bless the work",
To which he replied, "You too",
And said the shoe was for a Burke,
Who lived at a place called Cloonboo!

I said "what about this mountain dew,
You're supposed to have a jug nearby",
"Sure I thought you already knew,
'Twas the Breathalyser" he said with a sigh.

"Wasn't one of us sewing an upper
On a road down near Annaghdown,
The boot was for a man from Caherpucca",
Said he with a sorrowful frown!

"When up came a great big fellow
And sat him down on his knee,
Wearing a coat that was yellow
On the back it spelled out Gardai"!

I had to interrupt him there,
Saying "now you're telling me you're dry",
Says he "'tis true on my life I swear,
You know we fairies don't lie"!

The booze had made me a bit bold
And asked in a nice sort of way,
"Tell me about this pot of gold
You know what people here say"!

Said he "about this pot of gold money
Everything that's said is quite true,
They say we leprechauns are funny
Now it's the truth I'm telling you"!

"You'll get your crock of gold alright
But not until you get to the house,
And it will be shiny and bright,
So long as you don't wake the spouse"!

The road was in flood at the time
With water reaching the knee,
The cold and damp I didn't mind
I was only going to Canteeny!

There wasn't a light at the house
As usual she was upstairs in bed,
I tried to be as quiet as a mouse
But to be honest I'd waken the dead!

My wife is a nasty bit of work,
Her father came from Corofin,
He was one of the McGurks,
And her mother, was an O'Flynn!

Her sister was another bad penny
Who liked reading the Kama Suttra,
Until she married a fella called Kenny
And now lives in Mullacutra!

I remembered the day we married
She started to rant and to shout,
Our wedding was in a Tuam garage
That's why I couldn't back out!

She had locked me out I knew,
And shouted that I was cold,
And that it was really true
I was going to get a pot of gold!

Suddenly there was a noise at the window
It opened with a bang and a crash
And there was a flash of gold yellow
Which made one hell of a splash!

Didn't she swear and holler at me
Now wet and shivering cold,
She could be heard all over Canteeny,
Shouting, "there's your damned pot of gold!

The Coiste Bower

Come tonight the midnight hour
Will be seen and heard the Coiste Bower;
At haunting time it will appear
And men of Galway will shake in fear.

That phantom coach that fills with dread
Stalks the land carrying dead.
They who've seen it and lived to tell,
In shocking tones speak of hell!

Returning from pub, wake or spree
Sing and shout in revelry
But at sight of flaming wheels
Jump over walls or run through fields.

They talk of skeletons sitting inside
And headless horses with demon guides,
Of grown folk who in terror cower
At sight and sound of the Coiste Bower!

There are men with courage galore
Around Kiniska and Bawnmore,
Whether dancing a set or doing a jig,
Casting a cow or sticking a pig!

Yet at night when abroad alone
In dark boreens far from home
When comes the time of 'haunting hour'
Watch in fear for the Coiste Bower!

This ghostly hearse abroad will stray
And disappear at break of day,
When time is up for the travelling dead
For the Coiste Bower, it's home to bed!

Croagh Patrick

Let me once more climb that mountain,
And go again to the holy peak,
I hear the spirit calling,
Saying "last time to the reek".

To be a pilgrim just once more,
On St Patrick's blessed hill,
Where in youth I went before
When I was a Christian still.

Will that church on top
Nestling on the scree,
Open doors I so long closed,
Open again for me?

There I prayed long ago
In gales and pouring rain,
Tell me now you spirit,
Was this penance all in vain?

Tell me how I used my earthly time,
Was it honest and truly spent,
Tell me on this Mayo mountain,
Now on my last ascent?

When you came to utter prayer,
What were your thoughts within?
For Gods hand is everywhere
And also the hand of sin.

Do people come to praise God,
Or is it just an outing for the day.
Those who tread that holy sod
Have they too lost the way?

What you seek is not on the reek
Nor on mountains bleak and high,
Faith is a mystique that is unique,
Left abandoned it will die.

I cannot go to that mountain now
Where Patrick fasted for Lent,
But that closed door may open
For me, the one that says, repent.

Croagh Patrick: A place of pilgrimage in Co. Mayo where St Patrick fasted for forty days. It is an annual pilgrimage in July. The Reek: Another name for the mountain.

The Wind from Glennascaul

It was my time to forego sleep
In a field below the hill,
To keep a lambing watch on sheep,
When but a *putach* still.

A cold blast blew that ghostly night
Through my sheltering wall,
And I heard dead men in a fight,
On the wind from Glennascaul.

A sobbing cry of death and pain,
It was near and yet afar,
And men saying again and again,
Reideac, Reideac – na maraig an fear.

The struggle was all around me,
With the watching sheep intent,
Seeing what humans couldn't see –
That for the living wasn't meant.

I froze with terror in my youth,
For I was only a *putach* then,
Asking God in honest Truth,
Was I still with living men?

But God gave me no reply,
And didn't heed my tearful call,
Did he hear the dead men's cry,
On the wind from Glennascaul?

Morning came with welcome light,
Rousing me from that mereing wall,
Gone were the demons of the night –
And the wind from Glennascaul.

The Python Has It's Day

'T'wer on 'is Blackburn allotment
while working with hoe an't rake,
came on a great big serpent
that some folks now call a snake.

He knew that something wasn't reet
amongst greens an't curly kale,
t'wer nearly all of seventeen feet
from fangs to tip o' 'is tail!

He weren't going to argue with Python,
saying "reckon police knows best,
how to handle this 'ere Leviathan
asleep in't 'is chickens nest"!

Up came policeman in't van
saying "what's all this ballyhoo",
"yon snake has eaten our bantam",
said copper, "there's nowt I can do".

"I've seen some snakes in my time
but this is taking it too far,
when I were in't army front line
I saw things that were bizarre"!

"Why can't thee slit 'is stummick
and take out my bantam an veg",
said copper, "I'll tell ye summit,
it's to do with Safety and Regs"!

The gardener got all bothered and cross
an't snake was twitchy an't vexed,
said copper, "I'll have word with boss,
I'll just go send him a Text"!

But boss wer' of the old school
who'd felt many a collar in his day,
saying to 'is 'officer', don't be a fool,
Just phone up the RSPCA"!

They coiled up Python and took 'im away
with eyes all glittering bright
said copper, "I must get his DNA,
and then post im on't website.

From a press report - A snake ate chicken eggs from an allotment after being dumped by its keeper.

Flanders Trains

I hear marching footsteps fall
When I travel that War's terrain,
And sometimes too, bugle calls,
Onboard the Euro train.

The engine whistles loud at night,
Echoing over battlegrounds,
Where eager men went to fight,
Lonely – the locomotive sounds.

Proudly marching with heads high –
Slung rifles – pouches and packs,
And many now in Flanders lie,
Along these high speed tracks.

Did they hear artillery thunder
And fear the shells rain down,
Or join the many blown asunder –
Where Euro trains abound?

Once more I hear tramping feet
And see the Starshells shine –
As men retreat in fields of beet
Near the London Europe Line.

I close my eyes and listen again –
But it's only turning wheels,
Among growing crops of grain –
Now quiet are Flanders fields.

Places of legend and bloody battles,
And of angels in the sky –
Where now fast trains rattle,
And the dead forever lie.

To their Memory; the Connaught Rangers

The Somme Widow

I call your name to a distant sky,
You don't answer – there's No reply,
Oh my Bonnie lad in youthful bloom,
On bloody Somme met your doom.

I curse the day that you perished –
A soldiers' death with the Tyneside Irish;
Into 'no mans land's' thundering guns
Went men of Tyne and Erin's sons.

As 'over the top' you went in style,
Were your thoughts of the Emerald Isle,
Or on Shipyard, shop or Mine,
Wherein you toiled by Wear and Tyne?

Had you died by Shannon's wave,
Then we would have 'known your grave' –
Instead you lie on foreign Sod,
Of whom they say – Only known to God.

When to the land beyond the sky
I sometimes talk, and often cry,
And think of times short years ago,
When we were together here below.

Days of love, laughter and fun,
That went forever, on the Somme,
The Bairns and I now on our own,
And you Pet – a Name on Thiepval stone.

The 24th Tyneside Irish was part of the Northumberland Fusiliers formed after the outbreak of WWI. They were Irish or descendants, and first 'over the top' at the Somme 1st July 1916; and were decimated. Thiepval Memorial Records their names.

Sounds of Youth

I hear sounds through a window
Borne on winds that change,
The haunting sound of a mowing machine,
They're cutting hay in Grange.

Sometimes at night I lie awake
When fails the gift of sleep,
Once more I hear a corncrake
From meadows rich and deep.

Evocative was his echoing call
After the dawning day,
"Hurry up, hurry up" he's saying,
"Today they'll mow this hay".

Memories of youth come back
The sounds are with me still,
It's a threshing day in Lackaghbeg,
There's a distant droning mill.

I hear lapping waters
As the Clare flows gently by,
Our swimming pool by day,
By night our lullaby.

Winter's gone and the Cuckoo's song
Is heard above Knockdoe,
Telling Summer is here again
In Summers of long ago.

Far away a train is labouring
On Crumlins rail incline,
Trailing smoke and vapour,
Tomorrows weather will be fine.

St Bernards Well
On Knockroe of Old

In setting sun it's heathers glow,
God's own spotlight on Knockroe,
A flaming dress of embroidery
Beautiful then it was to see.

Our lovely hill in Heath attire
In evening light appeared on fire,
Getting its name – so people said –
Called Knockroe, the hill that's red.

From a distant train on the old railway
Echo's an Engine of the Mayo – Galway,
At Laraghs incline in labour strain
Whistling a lonely shrill refrain.

That trains whistle I hear it still
Reminding me again of Knockroe hill,
Imbibing water at St Bernard's Well,
That mankinds ailments could dispel.

Where pilgrims sometimes came to pray
For sin or sickness to allay,
Or reasons only they could tell –
You kept our secrets – St Bernard's Well.

Did they who sinned or pain endured,
Depart Knockroe healed and cured,
Was prayer and penance all in vain
Returning home as they came?

I saw faces going up the slope
On some there was no belief or hope,
In youthful days could not foresee
That one day too it would be me.

On my knees I prayed as well
And felt its water cast a spell,
Seeking what few could ever know –
And found the answer on Knockroe.

Around this world I've travelled wide,
Washing in waters of Ganges tide
And holy places where pilgrims throng –
Truly believing they'd got it wrong.

So much wanting to people tell,
What Bernard told me at his Well;
"Seek not for that you cannot find,
For all humanity – it's in the mind.

I love you dearly my Knockroe,
As I did long years ago,
And are you Bernard still in vogue,
Who stole my soul – you old rogue!

Lackagh of My Youth

Goodbye, goodbye dear Lackaghbeg, the place where I was born,
I'll never more see Lackagh Road, with its cattle, sheep and corn;
Fare thee well the Blacksmiths forge, the thatched cottages whence a boy,
I worked and played and often strayed, my heart so full of joy;
Many are the pails of water I fetched from the Poll Mor,
Hard did I toil on Irish soil, in those happy days of yore.

The bell rings out from Lackagh church, its strident tones so shrill,
And here a thousand miles away I swear I hear it still;
The Mass paths took the old and young and all who came to pray,
Come wet or dry, hail or snow, they never stayed away;
Is there mention of these people now, do we talk of them anymore?
Have they joined long gone dead, in the graveyard at Lackaghmore?

On Stephens day we took the wren, and went from door to door,
To Cahereenlea, via Cantoney, and through fields to Turloughmore;
Fond memories of my youth come back and sometimes causes pain,
The land where my forefathers lived and died, I'll never see again.

We went to the fair in Turloughmore, Oh what a wonderful day
And watched as enemies fought, and others joined the fray;
On we went to Jack Salac's Field, it caused our hearts to gladden,
And watched the latest cowboy film by courtesy of McFadden.
Farewell to Caheranoneen, Monard and Cahernahoon,
Goodbye to Ballinvoher, Coolarne and Ballyabrone.

Is the place of battle on the top of Knockdoe still?
Where Irishmen fought Irishmen up and down that hill;
Can be heard the ghostly clash, of battleaxe and spear,
Are wandering souls about who at night appear?

Softly flows the river Clare to the Corrib and the sea,
It goes along and sings a song only known to me,
It says you fools, I know your rules, there is no eternity,
Be as I, and just flow on and on, for I'm only a simple river,
Despite what all the world may say, I do not go on forever.

Adieu the land of my youth, the home of my cradle years,
At times the memories come flowing back, the toil, the fun, the tears:
Live for today, work and play, our thoughts now seem so shallow,
Our hopes and fears of bygone years should all be left to fallow.
The land we knew no longer exists, only thoughts and memories stay,
The people we loved are dead and gone, buried beneath the clay.

FOOD FOR THOUGHT

All this world I've travelled around
And such good food never found,
That in youth used to avail
The lovely taste of young lambs tail!

Who used to gambol just next day
After their tails were taken away,
Never thinking it wrong or cruel
Their appendage loss was non consensual!

Gathered up in sacks or pails
Lots and lots of young lambs tails,
In innocence didn't seem to mind
Their stumps soon healed in March wind!

And whilst around fields they ran
Their tails were in the frying pan,
Oh this dish was beyond compare
But for the lambs most unfair!

That we sat down inside to eat,
While they poor things were on their feet,
Wondering where their tails went
Removed from them without consent!

There never was such nice cuisine,
Second only to pigs crubeens,
What a treat when in the bog,
Cold lambs tails and feet of the hog!

Always a harbinger of Galway springs
Bainne bhui or beastings.
Honest and nourishing some used to maintain –
That buttermilk was Irish Champagne!

The author, Edward Coppinger in 1952